W9-BZC-364

S·C·H·O·L·A·S·T·I·C
MATH
PLACE™

REAL WORLD MATH FOR THINKING KIDS

Numbers, Numbers

Working With Larger Numbers to Describe What We Do

Published in cooperation with
Children Now
Oakland, California

Copyright © 1995 by Scholastic Inc.   All rights reserved. Published by Scholastic Inc.   Printed in U.S.A.
ISBN 0-590-27893-2
1 2 3 4 5 6 7 8 9 10   09   01 00 99 98 97 96 95 94

Numbers provide the language we use to count, describe, and compare quantities.

Numbers, Numbers

We count, add, subtract, and explore place value to gain
an understanding of larger numbers.

Video ▶

⋯⋯⋯⋯⋯⋯⋯⋯ ★ ᴿᴼᴹ ¹ ⋯⋯⋯⋯⋯⋯⋯⋯

SUBCONCEPT

We use numbers about ourselves to count,
add, and subtract.

⋯⋯⋯⋯⋯⋯⋯⋯⋯⋯⋯⋯⋯⋯⋯⋯⋯⋯⋯⋯⋯⋯

Big Book ▶

Read Aloud

SUBCONCEPT

2

We build larger numbers using repeated addition.

SUBCONCEPT

3

Using number patterns, we explore place value.

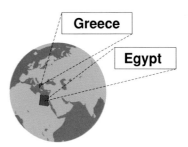

What Will Go in Your Number Almanac?

Fact: People started using almanacs over 3,000 years ago in ancient Egypt and Greece.

An almanac is a book of facts about almost everything, from animals with 4 noses to stars millions of miles away. A lot of the information is told with numbers. What facts tell about you?

Fact: My Classroom number
404

Fact: My Family
Me 7
Tom 13
Lisa 17
Jason 19

Fact: My phone number is
348-7432

Start an almanac.

DO·IT
- Make a record of the biggest numbers that describe you.
- Use them to make the cover of your almanac.

SHARE·IT
- Tell a partner one of your numbers.
- Have your partner guess what fact about you the number describes.

BUILD·ON·IT
- Which numbers show things you count? Which describe where you live or where you are?

You can use:
Paper
Pencil
Markers or crayons

THINK

Where do you see numbers in your school?

5

What Is the Longest Name in Your Class?

Fact: The longest name in the United States is shown on the birth certificate below.

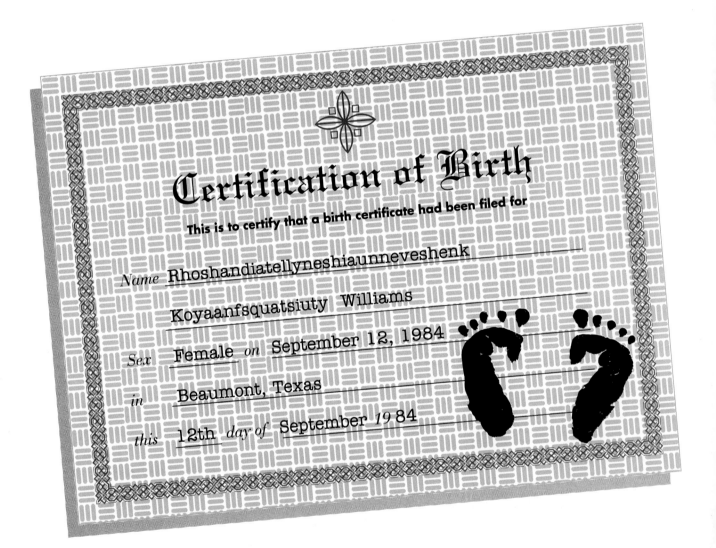

Certification of Birth

This is to certify that a birth certificate had been filed for

Name Rhoshandiatellyneshiaunneveshenk Koyaanfsquatsiuty Williams

Sex Female *on* September 12, 1984

in Beaumont, Texas

this 12th *day of* September 19 84

How long is your name? How can you find out?

Size up your name.

You can use:
- Paper
- Pencil
- Markers or crayons
- Calculator

DO·iT
- How many letters long is your first name? your last name?
- How long is your full name? Write this in your almanac. ✏

SHARE·iT
- Tell how you figured out the number of letters in your name?

BUILD·ON·iT
- Make a graph of the lengths of the names in your class.
- What is the most common number of letters in the names? ✏
- Which name is the longest?

First	Middle	Last
Leslie 6	Ann 3	Dann 4
Dorothy 7	Susan 5	Irwin 5
Brian 5	Wai 3	Lau 3
Nancy 5	Teresa 6	Soares 6
Ken 3	Adam 4	Barrios 7
Joseph 6	Dominic 7	Passalacqua 11

THINK

Which state has the longest name?

What Is the Most Expensive Name?

Fact: One of the most expensive autographs ever is on a letter signed by President Thomas Jefferson. It sold for $360,000.

Here is a game that lets you imagine how much your name is worth.

$360,000

Juan

$10 + 21 + 1 + 14$

$		$
A 1	N	14
B 2	O	15
C 3	P	16
D 4	Q	17
E 5	R	18
F 6	S	19
G 7	T	20
H 8	U	21
I 9	V	22
J 10	W	23
K 11	X	24
L 12	Y	25
M 13	Z	26

Play the autograph game.

DO·iT
- How much is your name worth? Use the letter price list to find out.
- Is your first or last name worth more? How much more ? ✏

You can use:
- Paper
- Pencil
- Calculator

SHARE·iT
- What name in your class is worth the most?
- Put the name in your almanac.

THINK

Why do you think Thomas Jefferson's autograph is worth so much money?

BUILD·ON·iT
- Flip the prices in the list. Make A worth $26 and Z worth $1. Can you guess what name is worth the most now? ✏

What Is the Longest Line That Will Fit in Your Classroom?

Fact: In an event called Hands Across America, people formed a line that stretched across America. The line was over 4,152 miles long.

What is the longest line you can make in your classroom?

Make the longest line.

You can use:
- Paper
- Pencil
- Calculator

DO·iT
- Line up with your class. How long a line can your class make?
- Estimate how many children it would take to go all the way around the classroom. Use the line your class made to help you.

SHARE·iT
- Share your estimate. Tell how you figured it out.

BUILD·ON·iT
- Estimate how many children it would take to make a line all around your school.

THINK
If you take a numbered ticket in a market, do you also have to stand in line? Why?

What Is the Fairest Way You Can Split Up Your Class?

Fact: The longest tug-of-war takes place across a bay in Michigan. Twenty people are needed on each team.

Tug-of-war is one of the oldest games around. Have you ever played it?

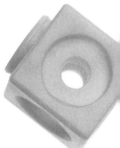

Make the fairest teams.

You can use:
- Cubes
- Paper
- Pencil

DO·IT
- Take cubes to represent the kids in your class.
- Make all the possible team combinations you can to play tug-of-war.

SHARE·IT
- Share your combinations.
- Which do you think are the most fair? Which are the least fair? Why?
- Put the fairest combinations in your almanac.

BUILD·ON·IT
- Find a way to organize your combinations.
- What patterns do you notice?

THINK

What part of an apple would you and a partner get if you each get a fair share of the apple?

13

How High Can You Count?

Fact: A googol is one of the biggest numbers that has a name.

What fact in your almanac has the biggest number?

Count as high as you can.

DO·iT
- Write down the biggest number you can count to.
- Try to find something with about that many things in your classroom.

SHARE·iT
- Count the things to show your number.
- What groupings make counting easier?

BUILD·ON·iT
- Write the biggest number you can count to in as many ways as you can.
- Put the number in your almanac.

You can use:
Classroom objects
Paper
Pencil

THINK
What is the quickest way of counting to 100?

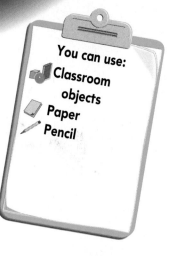

15

How Long Are You in School?

Fact: By the time you finish high school, you will have spent over 13,000 hours in school!

You go to school Monday through Friday. That's a good part of a week. How many hours do you think this is?

16

Figure out the time.

You can use:
- Paper
- Pencil
- Calculator

DO·iT
- Work with a partner. What time does school start each day? What time does school end?
- How many hours are you in school each day? each week?

SHARE·iT
- Show how you found your answers.

BUILD·ON·iT
- Imagine that you could go to school 24 hours a day.
- How many 24-hour days would you be in school each week? Use what you know about the hours you are in school to figure it out.

Week	Hours
Monday	6
Tuesday	6
Wednesday	
Thursday	
Friday	

THINK

About how many hours were you in school last month?

17

How Many Ways Can You Tell Your Age?

Fact: The oldest person on record was Shigechiyo Izumi of Japan. He lived about 120 years and 8 months.

People have different ways of telling their age. Most people give their age in years.

Find out your age in months.

You can use:
- Paper
- Markers or crayons
- Calculator
- Calendar

DO·it
- Draw a cake and decorate it with candles.
- Put on enough candles to show how many months old you are.

SHARE·it
- How many candles did you put on your cake?
- Tell how you figured it out.

BUILD·ON·it
- What are other ways you can tell how old you are?
- How exact can you be when telling your age?
- Put this age in your almanac.

Years	Months
1	12
2	24
3	

THINK

Why do we usually give our ages in years and not in months or weeks or days?

How Fast Can You Talk?

Fact: On a TV show called Motor Mouth, Steve Woodmore set the world's record for fast talking. He spoke about 637 words in one minute.

Are you a fast talker? It's not easy to talk fast and to speak clearly at the same time.

5 times
23 words

I have a dog
Her name is Savannah
How she loves to eat bananas
on the shores of Copacabana
with her best friend Hannah

Express yourself.

DO·iT
- Work with a partner. Pick a rhyme. Say the rhyme as fast as you can for 1 minute.
- How many times did you say the rhyme in 1 minute? How many words did you say?

You can use:
Rhyme
Stopwatch
Paper
Pencil
Calculator

SHARE·iT
- Compare your record with your partner's.

BUILD·ON·iT
- Now say the rhyme as slowly as you can. Keep track as before.
- What is the difference between your fastest and slowest records?

THINK

How fast does your heart beat in 1 minute? Find out.

How Can You Score 100 Points?

Fact: Wilt Chamberlain once scored 100 points in a basketball game. This is the greatest number of points scored by one player.

Here's a game you can play to try to score 100 points.

Race to 100.

DO·iT
- Play a game with a partner. Turn over one number card each.
- The player with the greater number gets to score the sum of the numbers.
- Make a tally of your points. Try to be the first to reach 100 points!

SHARE·iT
- How does tallying help you keep track of your points?

BUILD·ON·iT
- Play the game again. Keep score a different way. How does your new way of keeping score compare to making a tally chart?

You can use:
- 2 sets of number cards from 1-20
- Paper
- Pencil
- Calculator

THINK

How could you reach 100 points in just 3 turns?

What Number Patterns Can You Find?

Fact: In 1787, at the age of 10, Carl Friedrich Gauss correctly added all the numbers from 1 to 100 — in his head!

Did you know that finding number patterns can help you do math in your head?

Find patterns in a hundreds chart.

DO·IT

- Pick a number in the chart. What pattern do you see when you look down the column?
- What do you have to add to get each number?

SHARE·IT

- What if you had to add 11 to a number? How can the hundreds chart help you?

BUILD·ON·IT

- What other number patterns can you find in a hundreds chart?
- Try coloring in the numbers you say when you count by 2's or 5's.
- Tell about any patterns you find.

You can use:
Hundreds chart
Crayons
Paper
Pencil

THINK

How do patterns in addresses help a mail carrier deliver mail?

What Number Maze Can You Make?

Fact: The biggest maze in the world is in England. It is made of trees and has almost 2 miles of paths.

There are many different kinds of mazes. Some mazes can be made with numbers.

Find a number path.

DO·iT
- Play with a partner. Each pick two numbers on a hundreds chart. Try to make a path from one number to the other.
- Spin a spinner twice. Decide what 2-digit number will help you through the maze.
- Color that number on the chart.

You can use:
Hundreds chart
Spinner labelled 0-9
Markers or crayons
Calculator

SHARE·iT
- How did you decide what numbers to make?
- How are 31 and 13 different?

BUILD·ON·iT
- Use a calculator to find the sum of your path.

THINK
What path would have the largest sum?

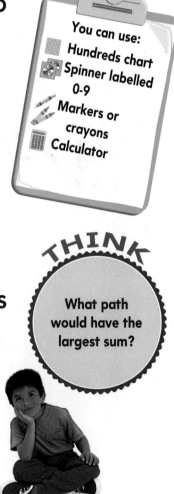

How Can You Solve a Number Puzzle?

Fact: The Rosetta stone helped people figure out Egyptian writing symbols. But it took almost 20 years to break the code!

You can use Egyptian number symbols to make number puzzles written in code.

You can use:

Paper

Pencil

Make a number puzzle.

DO·IT
- Write a fact puzzle about yourself using Egyptian numbers. You can write the numbers from right to left or from left to right.
- Ask a partner to solve it.

SHARE·IT
- Tell about the puzzle you solved.
- How are Egyptian numbers different from the numbers you use?

BUILD·ON·IT
- Write and solve more puzzles. Use Egyptian numbers and the numbers you usually use.

THINK

Besides I, ∩, ᕽ, what other numbers do you think there are Egyptian symbols for?

Which is greater?

∩∩∩II   or

40 - 3

What Can You Do With the Numbers in Your Almanac?

Fact: In 1889, the tallest tower was the Eiffel Tower at about 986 feet tall. Today, the tallest tower in the world is the CN Tower. It was built in 1975 and is about 1,815 feet tall.

You can compare facts you find in almanacs. What facts could you compare about these two towers?

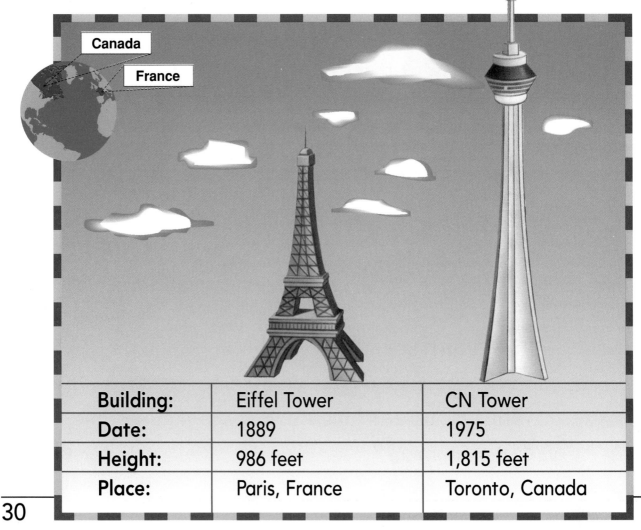

Building:	Eiffel Tower	CN Tower
Date:	1889	1975
Height:	986 feet	1,815 feet
Place:	Paris, France	Toronto, Canada

Josh
82 months old

91-82=

Maia
91 months old

Share your facts.

DO·iT • Work with a partner. Choose the same fact from your almanacs.
• Write a problem using the numbers in your facts. Solve it.

You can use:
Paper
Pencil
Markers or crayons
Calculator

SHARE·iT • Tell how you solved your problem. Did you add or subtract? Did you compare?

THINK

What number problem can you write that has an answer of 10?

BUILD·ON·iT • Write and solve more problems using facts from your almanacs. What different kinds of problems can you write?

31

What Are Your Favorite Facts in the Almanac?

Pick the facts that you like best. Show their numbers in as many ways as you can.